Published by Creative Medicine: Healing Through Words,

PO Box 2749, Tappahannock, VA, 22560

Copyright© 2018 by Creative Medicine: Healing Through Words, LLC

All rights reserved. Educator's Guide to the Nelson Beats the Odds Series (including prominent characters featured in this issue), its logo and all character likeness are trademarks of Creative Medicine: Healing Through Words, LLC, unless otherwise noted. No part of this publication may be reproduced or transmitted, in any form or by any means (except for short excerpts for review purposes), electronic or mechanical, including photocopy, or any information storage and retrieval system, without permission from the publisher.

All names, events and locales in this publication are entirely fictional.

ISBN 978-978-099-005-3 (Paperback)

ISBN 978-978-099-006-0 (Paperback)

Author: Ronnie Sidney, II, LCSW

Designer: Kurt Keller

Illustrator: Traci Van Wagoner

Editors: Charles Barrett, Krystle Bradley, Tiffany Day, Boyd George, and Yanna Spellman

PRINTED IN THE USA

Please visit www.nelsonbeatstheodds.com for information about Educator's Guide to the Nelson Beats the Odds Series, Rest in Peace RaShawn Reloaded, Nelson Beats the Odds, Tameka's New Dress, Nelson Beats the Odds Comic Creator app, and mix-tape. Follow us on social media and use the hashtag #RIPrashawn, #TamekasNewDress, #NelsonBeatsTheOdds, #NBTO and #iBeatTheOdds.

 @ronniesidneyii   @nelsonbeatstheo @ronniesidneyi

 Ronnie Sidney, II, LCSW

Creative Medicine: Healing Through Words, LLC

CONTENTS

EDUCATOR'S GUIDE TO THE NELSON BEATS THE ODDS SERIES

Table of Contents

- I. Overview..6
    1. General objectives for educator's guide
    2. General objectives for classroom activities
    3. General information about our services and products

- II. Graphic Novels..17
    1. The Three E's of Comics by Josh Elder
    2. Diversity in children's books
    3. Depictions of disability in media
    4. Diverse books that feature characters with disabilities
    5. Discussion questions
    6. Sources and other supplemental information

- III. Learning and Attention Issues...................................20
    1. What are learning and attention issues?
    2. What are signs of learning and attention issues?
    3. Misconceptions about learning and attention issues
    4. Three things you need to know about learning disabilities
    5. Engaging families in special education services
    6. Disproportionality
    7. Racial disparities in special education
    8. What is inclusion?
    9. Four principles of effective inclusion
    10. Inclusion and federal law

11. How can educators help children and families beat the odds?

12. Discussion questions

13. Sources and other supplemental information

IV. Cultural Responsiveness..25

1. Can teachers' beliefs and expectations influence student success?

2. Implicit and explicit bias

3. Cultural responsiveness inventory

4. Microaggressions

5. Examples of microaggressions in the classroom

6. What can educators do to decrease microaggressions and bias?

7. Discussion questions

8. Sources and other supplemental information

V. Trauma..30

1. What is trauma?

2. Trauma and the brain

3. Trauma's impact on education and behavior

4. Recognizing child abuse and neglect

5. Trauma informed schools

   A. A program, organization, or system that is trauma-informed

   B. Classroom elements to avoid

   C. How to approach individuals who have experienced trauma

   D. Six ways to become a trauma-informed school by the National Resilience Institute

   E. Ten tips for managing escalating behaviors at school

   F. Ways educators can support youth who have experienced trauma

   G. How to approach individuals who have experienced trauma

6. Discussion questions

7. Sources and other supplemental information

VI. Grief and Loss..**37**
   1. What is grief?
   2. Stages of grief
   3. Ways to support someone who is experiencing grief and loss
   4. Expressions of grief
   5. Spirituality and grief
   6. What should I say to a student who is experiencing grief?
   7. Discussion questions
   8. Sources and other supplemental information

VII. Bullying..**42**
   1. What is bullying?
   2. Verbal, relational, and physical bullying
   3. Discussion questions
   4. Sources and other supplemental information

VIII. Gangs..**45**
   1. Warning signs your students may be in a gang
   2. Five reasons why young people join gangs
   3. What can educators do to prevent gang involvement?
   4. Discussion questions
   5. Sources and other supplemental information

IX. Self-Care..**48**
   1. 12 stages of burnout
   2. Compassion fatigue
   3. Stress reduction kit
   4. Self-care tips
   5. 30 self-care activities for educators
   6. Discussion questions
   7. Sources and other supplemental information

X. Student Activities..53

    1. How to taste a book

    2. Matching activity

    3. Somebody wanted but so then

    4. Character on a roll

    5. Character profile

    6. Word search

    7. What I think about a book

    8. Action poster

XI. Book List..64

XII. Additional Resources..66

    1. Trauma

    2. Learning disabilities

    3. Teacher resources

    4. Emotional and behavior disorders

    5. Attention deficit disorder/attention-deficit/hyperactivity disorder

    6. Legal/advocacy information and resources

    7. Visual impairment

    8. Gangs

    9. Books

OVERVIEW

It is critical that our nation's schools support students with disabilities in the classroom, but it is equally essential that we understand how to work with diverse students who've experienced trauma and grief. To promote students' academic success and well-being, we must create inclusive, culturally responsive, trauma-informed environments. *The Educator's Guide to the Nelson Beats the Odds Series* presents recommendations for eight leadership competencies to guide educators as they integrate *Nelson Beats the Odds*, *Tameka's New Dress*, and *Rest in Peace RaShawn Reloaded* into their classroom curriculum. *The Guide* was developed by award-winning author and therapist, Ronnie Sidney II, LCSW and illustrated by Imagine That! Design.

The Guide provides educators with practical strategies to promote positive student outcomes and increased emotional well-being. *The Guide* will provide students with activities to facilitate the reflection and interpretation of themes and ideas associated with the *Nelson Beats the Odds* graphic novel series. Educators will be provided with practical strategies to help them improve school success for students with learning and attention issues and students with trauma histories.

The Educator's Guide to the Nelson Beats the Odds Series includes tips for working with students who have:

- Unresolved trauma
- Physical disabilities
- Reading difficulties
- Poor attention spans
- Poor organization skills
- Poor social skills
- Aggression and anger
- Bullying tendencies
- Grief and loss
- Gang affiliation

The Guide will explore how educators can better support diverse students and individuals with learning and attention issues.

General objectives for Educator's Guide

Educators will:

- Gain knowledge and understanding about graphic novels, disabilities, trauma, and contemporary issues, especially in terms of how educators can better support a growing number of diverse students.

- Strengthen their ability to work with students with disabilities and with trauma histories, and be able to identify the intersections of ability, race, and gender.

- Learn to examine bias, microaggressions, and cultural responsiveness and discuss how these elements shape schools and classrooms.

- Demonstrate improved skills in analyzing the *Nelson Beats the Odds Series* and effectively utilize *The Educator's Guide* to enhance students' critical thinking skills.

General objectives for classroom activities

In each of the five literacy explorations, students will:

- Learn age-appropriate information about learning disabilities, trauma, grief, gangs, and bullying.

- Build critical thinking skills by completing puzzles, quizzes and discussion questions about the graphic novel.

- Practice reading strategies and skills needed to decode and comprehend the graphic novels.

- Connect to personal experiences that shape resilience and grit.

- Improve cultural awareness by exploring empowering stories about underrepresented groups.

General information about our services and products

Creative Medicine: Healing Through Words, LLC (CMHTW) was founded by Ronnie Nelson Sidney, II, LCSW in 2015. Creative Medicine: Healing Through Words began as an expressive writing group for adult male offenders at the Northern Neck Regional Jail in Warsaw, Virginia. The company's mission is to improve participants' social, emotional and physical health outcomes through therapeutic writing and dialogue. CMHTW envisions a world where people will use therapeutic writing and dialogue as tools to restore hope and heal wounds.

Our highly qualified facilitators are skilled and experienced at working with individuals from diverse populations. We offer professional development workshops, author visits, school assemblies, book talks, book readings, therapeutic writing and dialogue workshops.

DIVERSE GRAPHIC NOVEL SERIES
INSPIRES KIDS TO BEAT THE ODDS

"Engaging and inspirational tales for students coping with common problems." — Kirkus Review

"What wonderful surprises all these books bring."— Nikki Giovanni

These are just the books to put into the hands of a struggling child.

Our books help young people...
- Improve cultural awareness and literacy skills.
- Connect to personal experiences that shape resilience and grit.
- Improve self-esteem by providing empowering images of underrepresented groups.
- Explore trauma, learning disabilities, and bullying with a gentle touch.

RONNIE SIDNEY, II, LCSW, a Virginia native, is an award-winning author, professional speaker and licensed therapist. In third grade, the author-therapist was diagnosed with a learning disability and spent seven years in special education. Sidney's early academic challenges ignited a passion within him to pursue social justice and to work with the youth. After graduating Virginia Commonwealth University in 2014, Sidney went on to self-publish Nelson Beats the Odds, Tameka's New Dress, Nelson Beats the Odds: Compendium One, Rest in Peace RaShawn and Rest in Peace RaShawn Reloaded. In 2015, Sidney helped develop the Nelson Beats the Odds Comic Creator self-esteem app.

Ronnie Sidney, II, LCSW has over a decade of experience speaking at schools, colleges, churches, and conferences. His presentations focus on resilience, disabilities, trauma, cultural responsiveness, resilience, and more. Email inquiries to nelsonbeatstheodds@gmail.com.

Professional Speaker Services	**Fee Schedule**	**Time Allotted**
School Visits, Book Talks and Book Readings	$750 - $5,000	4 hours
Professional Development Workshops	$1,500 - $10,000	4 hours
Keynote and Conference Presentations	$1,500 - $15,000	4 hours

Travel and lodging fees apply for events 90 miles or more outside of Tappahannock, Virginia. Each additional hour beyond the allotted time will require an additional $300 per hour fee. Video conferencing services are available for a discounted rate.

Speaker Topics:

- The Journey from a Child with Learning and Attention Issues to a Best-Selling Author
- A Story of Resilience: How I Beat the Odds
- Helping our most Vulnerable Children Beat the Odds
- How can I Help: Doing Life with Learning and Attention Issues
- Is your Organization Trauma-Informed and Culturally Responsive?
- Perceptions of the Black Father
- Liberty and Justice for All? Examining the Untold Trayvon Martin Stories

Ronnie Sidney, II, LCSW's trinity of quality, young adult literature, includes *Nelson Beats the Odds*, *Tameka's New Dress*, and *Rest in Peace RaShawn Reloaded*. All three graphic novels inspire confidence in children, especially children of color, and encourage a fondness for reading and a heightened level of social awareness. Sidney's stories present learning disabilities, trauma, and bullying in a sensitive, easy-to-understand and age-appropriate format for kids. *Untold Narratives: African Americans Who Received Special Education Services and Succeeded Beyond Expectations* documents Sidney's childhood experience in one of its chapters.

Books	Retail Rate	Bulk Discount
Nelson Beats the Odds	$15	$8
Rest in Peace RaShawn Reloaded	$15	$8
Tameka's New Dress	$15	$8
Nelson Beats the Odds: Compendium One	$20	$10
Untold Narratives: African Americans Who Received Special Education Services and Succeeded Beyond Expectations	$45	$40
Nelson Beats the Odds Activity Guide	$20	$10
Educator's Guide to the Nelson Beats the Odds Series	$35	$20

Photo Credit: Tawaan Brown
Features: Ronnie Sidney, II, LCSW and Jennifer Veney

NELSON BEATS THE ODDS

F&P Text Level Gradient: T

Grade Level Equivalent: 5

Interest Level by Grade: 4 and up

Educational Description: Book 1: *Nelson Beats the Odds Series*, Realistic fiction, graphic/comic format, informational side text; quotes, facts.

Story elements: Setting, plot and character development, problem and solution, cause and effect relationships, figurative language; simile, illustrations enhance meaning and tone.

Theme and ideas: Learning disabilities, ADHD, school, friendship, resilience, setting goals.

Book Summary: Nelson used to think school was all about playing around and talking with his friends. When Nelson learns that he's been placed in special education, he fears being teased so he keeps his learning disability and ADHD diagnosis a secret. With the encouragement of his parents and assistance from Mrs. T., his special education teacher, Nelson pushes the boundaries and discovers his potential. *Nelson Beats the Odds* is an Amazon Best-Selling graphic novel.

TAMEKA'S NEW DRESS

F&P Text Level Gradient: W

Grade Level Equivalent: 6

Interest Level by Grade: 4 and up

Educational Description: Book 2: *Nelson Beats the Odds Series*, Realistic fiction, graphic/comic format, poetry: point of view; main character, Tameka, informational side text; quotes, facts.

Story elements: Setting, plot and character development, author's purpose, problem and solution, cause and effect relationships, changes from beginning to end of the story, illustrations enhance meaning and tone.

Theme and ideas: Social issues- racial diversity/inequality, abuse, bullying, family, friendship, conflict resolution.

Book Summary: When you're the new girl in school it can be a little scary. It's even tougher when your parents aren't there to help. Some of the kids might be friendly but what about that mean girl who's always picking on you? The author brings up the subjects of childhood trauma, parental substance abuse, kinship care and bullying with a gentle touch suitable for even the youngest children. *Tameka's New Dress* shines a light on these tough things and lays them out on the table to talk about. He also presents us with a strong girl in Tameka, who not only finds adults who can and do support her, but also finds a way to confront her bullies without becoming a bully herself. Real tips for real life situations are presented here – just what real little children need - a great addition to the library shelves.

5 REAL-LIFE BLACK WOMEN WHO INFLUENCED TAMEKA'S NEW DRESS

CHERLANDA SIDNEY-ROSS- is a Program Specialist for the Virginia Department of Social Services. She is a graduate of Virginia Commonwealth University (VCU). Cherlanda is sister of Ronnie Sidney, II, LCSW, author of the *Nelson Beats the Odds Series*. She is featured as a social worker in *Tameka's New Dress* and rescues the Tameka from her chaotic home environment.

QUEEN NEFERTITI- is the wife of one of the most famous pharaohs of ancient Kemet, also known as Egypt, Akhenaten. Sidney named Kemet Middle School in *"Tameka's New Dress"* after ancient Kemet. Pharaoh Akhenaten and Queen Nefertiti began a religious revolution in Kemet called the cult of Aten. The two influenced contemporary religions like Christianity and Judaism. After Nefertiti's husband died, scholars believe she ruled Kemet as Neferneferuaten.

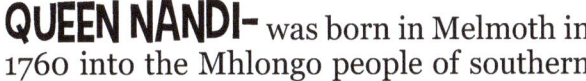

QUEEN NANDI- was born in Melmoth in 1760 into the Mhlongo people of southern Africa. She was mother of Shaka, king of Zulus. Queen Nandi had to protect her son from famine and assassination attempts. Through Queen Nandi's strength, Shaka learned great power and resistance. She encouraged her son never settle for less, which would result in a thriving kingdom.

NZINGA MBANDE- more commonly known as Queen Anna Nzinga, lived from 1581-1663 and ruled the Ndongo and Matamba Kingdoms. Queen Nzinga was born into a ruling family and demonstrated a unique ability to defuse political crises at a young age. Most known for being a strong military leader, Queen Nzinga led her kingdoms by fighting the slave trade and leading the resistance against the Portuguese.

SANDRA BLAND- was a 28-year-old Black woman from Naperville, Illinois. She was found hanged in a jail cell in Waller County, Texas, on July 13, 2015, three days after being arrested during a traffic stop. Sandra was a critic of police brutality and an advocate for social justice. Bland Middle School in *Nelson Beats the Odds* is named after Sandra Bland.

Above Photo Credit: Virginia Commonwealth University
Features: Cherlanda Sidney-Ross

Right Photo Credit: Sandra Bland
Features: Sandra Bland

REST IN PEACE RASHAWN RELOADED

F&P Text Level Gradient: Z+

Grade Level Equivalent: High School

Interest Level By Grade: 8 and up

Educational Description: Book 3: *Nelson Beats the Odds Series*, Realistic fiction; graphic/comic format, Questions and answers based on real interviews.

Story elements: Setting, plot and character development, problem and solution, cause and effect relationships, Illustrations enhance meaning and tone: dark.

Themes and ideas: Social issues; racial diversity/ inequality, street violence; gangs, police involved shootings, loss, community.

Book Summary: *Rest in Peace RaShawn Reloaded* is more than the story of an accidental shooting. It's the vivid story of a young man's life snuffed out too soon by police bullets – a narrative that, sadly, has become all too familiar in America.

The author, Ronnie Sidney, II, LCSW captures the emotional upheaval suffered by families and communities nationwide following the sudden, violent demise of black men. He presents the violence and suffering in a sensitive, easy-to-understand and age-appropriate format for kids. This book is a good way to broach the painful but necessary conversations families across the nation are having with their children, and provides thoughtful discussion points on how to heal the legacy of distrust between African- American communities and the police who are supposed to protect them. *Rest in Peace ReShawn Reloaded* was selected for the Recommended Book List for the 2018 In the Margins Book Award. A committee of librarians who work with marginalized youth decided Ronnie's book was an outstanding fit to recommend to other groups who work with marginalized youth. *Rest in Peace ReShawn Reloaded* was also an honorable mention award winner for the 2018 Young Adult Virginia Authors (YAVA) award.

Critically Acclaimed Novels Help Young Adults Explore Race and Police Brutality

The rise of police violence against Black and Hispanic teenagers is alarming. Authors Ronnie Sidney, II, Monique Morris, Angie Thomas, and Jason Reynolds seek to confront police brutality by providing well-written and exciting stories for young adult readers.

THE HATE U GIVE by Angie Thomas

"Sixteen-year-old Starr Carter moves between two worlds: the poor neighborhood where she lives and the fancy suburban prep school she attends. The uneasy balance between these worlds is shattered when Starr witnesses the fatal shooting of her childhood best friend Khalil at the hands of a police officer. Khalil was unarmed.

Soon afterward, his death is a national headline. Some are calling him a thug, maybe even a drug dealer and a gangbanger. Protesters are taking to the streets in Khalil's name. Some cops and the local drug lord try to intimidate Starr and her family. What everyone wants to know is: what really went down that night?"

ALL AMERICAN BOYS by Jason Reynolds and Brendan Keily

"A 2016 Coretta Scott King Author Honor book, and recipient of the Walter Dean Myers Award for Outstanding Children's Literature.

In this Coretta Scott King Honor Award–winning novel, two teens—one black, one white—grapple with the repercussions of a single violent act that leaves their school, their community, and, ultimately, the country bitterly divided by racial tension.

A bag of chips. That's all sixteen-year-old Rashad is looking for at the corner bodega. What he finds instead is a fist-happy cop, Paul Galluzzo, who mistakes Rashad for a shoplifter, mistakes Rashad's pleadings that he's stolen nothing for belligerence, mistakes Rashad's resistance to leave the bodega as resisting arrest, mistakes Rashad's every flinch at every punch the cop throws as further resistance and refusal to STAY STILL as ordered. But how can you stay still when someone is pounding your face into the concrete pavement?

There were witnesses: Quinn Collins—a varsity basketball player and Rashad's classmate who has been raised by Paul since his own father died in Afghanistan—and a video camera. Soon the beating is all over the news and Paul is getting threatened with accusations of prejudice and racial brutality. Quinn refuses to believe that the man who has basically been his savior could possibly be guilty. But then Rashad is absent. And absent again. And again. And the basketball team—half of whom are Rashad's best friends—start to take sides. As does the school. And the town. Simmering tensions threaten to explode as Rashad and Quinn are forced to face decisions and consequences they had never considered before."

PUSHOUT by Monique M. Morris

"Fifteen-year-old Diamond stopped going to school the day she was expelled for lashing out at peers who constantly harassed and teased her for something everyone on the staff had missed: she was being trafficked for sex. After months on the run, she was arrested and sent to a detention center for violating a court order to attend school.

Just 16 percent of female students, Black girls make up more than one-third of all girls with a school-related arrest. The first trade book to tell these untold stories, Pushout exposes a world of confined potential and supports the growing movement to address the policies, practices, and cultural illiteracy that push countless students out of school and into unhealthy, unstable, and often unsafe futures."

Other notable books that confront the epidemic of police violence

Include the following:

- Tyler Johnson Was Here by Jay Coles
- Dear Martin by Nic Stone
- I Am Alfonso Jones by Tony Medina and
    Illustrated by John Jennings and Stacey Robinson
- Ghost Boys by Jewell Parker Rhodes
- How It Went Down by Kekla Magoon
- Between the World and Me by Ta-Nehisi Coates
- They Can't Kill Us All by Wesley Lowery

Photo Credit: Kelsee Scott, Kelsee Scott Portraits LLC
Featured: Ronnie Sidney, II, LCSW, Mali Self, Talisha Sidney, and Morgan Self.

GRAPHIC NOVELS

Graphic novels are stories written and illustrated in rich, lively visuals with a limited amount of text. The illustrations are presented in rectangular patterns and the story unfolds in clear, often action-packed sequence. Graphic novels range from science fiction to historical nonfiction. The *Nelson Beats the Odds Series* is proof main characters do not have to be superheroes. This section will explore graphic novels, diversity, and depictions of disabilities in the media.

Graphic novels...

- Encourage us to question, challenge, and re-think how we look at the world.
- Are edifying to children.
- Are great platforms to address social justice issues.
- Offer well-written and exciting stories, new points of view and stimulating artwork.
- Appeal to a wide audience of readers.
- Provide positive, empowering images of underrepresented groups.
- Attract reluctant readers i.e. middle school & minority boys.

The Three E's of Comics by Josh Elder

- Engagement: Graphic novels draw readers in because they find the accompanying artwork appealing and the stories engaging. Comics actively engage readers, imparting meaning with written language, and juxtaposed sequential images. Decoding text enables individuals to read more complex stories than is possible with traditional illustrations and text. Readers actively make meaning from the interplay of images and text, as well as by filling in the gaps between panels.

- Efficiency: The comic format conveys large amounts of information in a short time. This is especially effective when working with struggling and emergent readers. The efficiency also helps when teaching content in the subject areas (math, science, social studies, etc.).

- Effectiveness: Processing images and text together leads to better transfer of learning and recall. The Dual-Coding Theory of Cognition explained that we process text and images in different areas of the brain. The neurological experiments indicate that pairing a text with an image leads to increased memory retention for both. With comics, students not only learn the material better, they learn it faster.

Diversity in children's books

- In 2016, the number of diverse books being published jumped to 28%. This year 31% books covered were diverse, making it the highest on record since 1994.

- The number of books written by people of color hasn't changed much since 2016. African-American, Latin, and Native authors combined wrote just 6% of new children's books published. In 2017 the number was only 7%.

- A majority of books (diverse or not) are written by white authors.

- We Need Diverse Books™ international campaign promotes books that reflect and honor the lives of young people.

Depictions of disability in media

Biklen and Bogdan identified ten major stereotypes commonly used in media to portray individuals with disabilities.

- Pitiable and pathetic- Tiny Tim in A Christmas Carol.

- Object of violence- Audrey Hepburn's character who is terrorized as an individual who is blind in the movie —"Wait Until Dark".

- Sinister and/or evil- Captain Ahab w/ one prosthetic leg.

- Atmospheric- Individuals who are background characters.

- Super Crip- The private detective who used a wheelchair.

- Laughable- Mr. Magoo, who had a visual impairment.

- Burden- Characters who appear as being helpless, in need of care.

- Nonsexual- Those who appear —as totally incapable of sexual activity.

- Incapable of fully participating in everyday life- Those who are presented as unable to be included in activities as employees, brothers or sisters, students, etc.

Diverse books that feature students with disabilities

- El Deafo by CeCe Bell

- Out of my Mind by Sharon M. Draper

- My Brother Charlie by Holly Robinson Peete and Ryan Elizabeth Peete

- We're Amazing 1, 2, 3! A Story about Friendship and Autism by Leslie Kimmelman and Beth Nelson

- What it's Like to be me is illustrated and written by children with disabilities

- Willy's Summer Dream by Kay Brown
- Front of the Class by Brad Cohen
- Mrs. Gorski, I Think I Have The Wiggle Fidgets by Barbara Esham
- Meet Clarabelle Blue by Adiba Nelson, Elvira Morando, and Ilene Serna
- We'll Paint the Octopus Red by Stephanie Stuve Booden and Pam Devito

Discussion questions

1. Gather a collection of diverse graphic novels. Introduce them to your students and ask them how they are different from other books. During the discussion, find the right moment to introduce illustrations, dialogue, speech bubbles, and more.

Sources and other supplemental information

1. "Comics in the Classroom: Why Comics?" by Michelle Manno-https://teach.com/blog/why-comics/
2. "Nelson Beats the Odds: Author of the ADHD Comic on the Power of Encouragement" by Cathy Vandewater- https://teach.com/blog/nelson-beats-the-odds/
3. "Seeing the Same: A Follow-Up Study on the Portrayals of Disability in Graphic Novels Read by Young Adults" by Robin Moeller and Marilyn Irwin- http://www.ala.org/aasl/sites/ala.org.aasl/files/content/aaslpubsandjournals/slr/vol15/SLR_SeeingtheSame_V15.pdf
4. "The diversity gap in children's book publishing, 2018" by Jalissa Corrie- http://blog.leeandlow.com/2018/05/10/the-diversity-gap-in-childrens-book-publishing-2018/

LEARNING AND ATTENTION ISSUES

Nelson Beats the Odds is a story about Nelson, a fifth grader at Bland Middle School. Nelson is placed in special education after he is diagnosed with ADHD and a learning disability. Nelson keeps his learning disability and ADHD diagnosis a secret because he fears being teased. Ronnie Nelson Sidney II, LCSW, author of *Nelson Beats the Odds*, also struggled with the stigma of being placed in special education. He was diagnosed as learning disabled (dysgraphia and ADHD), spending seven years in special education. Ronnie's real-life experiences inspired Nelson's character.

This section will explore learning and attention issues, inclusion and strategies educators could use to join with students with disabilities and their families.

What are learning and attention issues?

- Also known as brain-based difficulties, they can cause kids to struggle in school, at home, socially, and with everyday skills.
- Common learning and attention issues include dyslexia, dysgraphia, dyspraxia, ADHD, ADD, and executive functioning skills.
- They often run in families and are not the result of where or how a child grows up.

What are signs of learning and attention issues?

- Particular difficulty in an academic study or organization.
- Not wanting to go to school.
- Taking a long time to do routine homework.
- Having a disorganized backpack.
- Having messy handwriting.

Misconceptions about learning and attention issues

- Having a learning and attention issue does not mean a child isn't intelligent.
- Twice Exceptional (2e) students are intellectually gifted children who have some form of disability.
- Some parents think learning and attention issues are caused by poor diets, vaccinations, or too much television.Lack of parent or teacher involvement in early childhood can cause learning and attention issues.

- The child is being lazy

Three things you ned to know about learning disabilities

- One in five people have a learning or attention issue.

- Having learning and attention issues doesn't mean a child isn't intelligent.

- Understood.org offers support, a sense of community, and expert information for parents of children with learning and attention issues.

Engaging families in special education services

Educators will:

- Remember individuals and families are the experts; educators are seen as consultants.

- Have mutual respect, joint decision-making, sharing of feelings, flexibility, and honestly in dealing with each other.

- Meet the needs of the system at their pace.

- Be knowledgeable and well-informed about services and resources available.

- Connect individuals and families to others with similar experiences.

- Maintain consistency and follow-up in timely manner; time is valuable to everyone.

- Focus on the individual's best interest and focus on what's right not who's right.

- Seek supervision and guidance when faced with challenging situations.

Disproportionality

Disproportionality refers to the underrepresentation or overrepresentation of a particular demographic group in special education programs relative to the presence of this group in the overall student population. Race and ethnicity have a significant influence on the probability a student will be misidentified as needing special education services. Misidentified special education students receive unwarranted services and supports and are likely to encounter limited access to rigorous curricula. Lower teacher expectations and social stigma contribute to diminished academic performance and post-secondary opportunities for students with disabilities.

Racial disparities in special education

- African-American students are referred for special education programs more often for emotional disabilities and described as having challenging behaviors.

- African-American and Hispanic students continue to be overrepresented in special education, have higher dropout rates, and are suspended and expelled at higher rates than their peers.

- American Indian/Alaska Native children receive special education services at twice the rate of the general student population.

- Asian and Pacific Islander students are overesented in gifted and talented programs but are less likely to be identified for special education.

- School districts with relatively small English-language learners (ELL) populations are more likely to receive special education services than in districts with large populations.

What is inclusion?

Inclusion is the belief that all children are included for all or part of the day in the general education setting with their needs met. Treating special education students equitably in classrooms or environments prepare them for success. Inclusion helps improve students' academic, behavioral, self-esteem and social skills with appropriate supports.

Four principles of effective inclusion

- **Diversity**-Effective inclusion improves the educational system for all students by placing them together in general education classroom- regardless of their learning ability, race, linguistic ability, economic status, gender, learning style, ethnicity, cultural background, religion, family structure and sexual orientation.

- **Individual Needs**-Effective inclusion involves sensitivity to and acceptance of individual needs and differences.

- **Reflective Practice**-Effective inclusion requires reflective educators to modify their attitudes, teaching and classroom management practices, and curricula to accommodate individual needs.

- **Collaboration**-Effective inclusion is a group effort; it involves collaboration among educators, other professionals, students, families, and community agencies.

Inclusion and federal law

- The Individuals with Disabilities Education Act (IDEA) was enacted in 1975 and mandates a public education for all eligible children and the school's responsibility for providing the supports and services that will allow this to happen.

- The American with Disabilities Act of 1990 (ADA) sets forth protections and provisions for equal access to education for anyone with a disability.

- IDEA provides for a "free appropriate public education" (FAPE) for all children with disabilities, entitling them to an education that is tailored to their special needs. At no cost to the family.

- IDEA provides that students with disabilities are entitled to experience the "least restrictive environment" (LRE).

- School districts are required to educate students with disabilities in regular classrooms with non-disabled peers, in the school they would attend if not disabled, to the maximum extent appropriate, and supported with aids/services to make this possible.

- The Individualized Education Plan (IEP) is the document that spells out the student's needs and how they will be met.

How can educators help children and families beat the odds?

Educators will:

- Provide early and effective educational interventions.

- Develop an inclusive learning environment that helps SPED students maximize their strengths.

- Help educate children and families on the signs of learning and attention issues and understanding of the diagnosis if there is one.

- Support them in overcoming the stigma of special education services.

- Empower students and families by giving them opportunities to self-determine.

- Help them form a community of individuals who share common experiences.

- Provide resources for parents and support them in advocating for their children.

- Assist the family in developing a supportive home and school environment so their children can thrive.

Discussion questions

1. What are some successful strategies you used to work with students with learning and attention issues?

2. What are the biggest challenges you face?

3. How can you and your school better support students with learning and attention issues?

4. This activity is designed for you to see your special education students in a different light. Ask them the following questions individually or in a group.

    1. Complete the sentence stem "I am…"

    2. How old were you and how did you feel when you qualified for special education services?

    3. Do you feel embarrassed about receiving special education services? How can your teachers help you feel more comfortable?

4. What are some things about you that you wished your teachers knew?

5. What are your special education accommodations? How do you feel about using them?

6. How do your classmates react to you using your IEP accommodations in the general education setting?

7. How does your IEP impact you academically?

8. What are some things you do well?

Sources and other supplemental information

1. Wrightslaw- http://www.wrightslaw.com/

2. Understood- http://www.understood.org

3. National Center for Learning Disabilities- https://www.ncld.org/

4. "How Ronnie Sidney Beat the Odds" by Judy Brenis- https://add.org/beat-the-odds/

5. "Autism and School Inclusion" by Mojan Pourmand, Psy.D.

Cultural Responsiveness

Culturally responsive teachers recognize the importance of including students' cultural identity in all aspects of enriching classroom experiences. Teachers who practice cultural responsiveness keep their students engaged and enhance their educational journey. According to Dr. Zakia Gates, culturally responsive educators are aware of the "linguistic, academic, emotional, and social development of that person, especially our African-American children in our schools."

The National Association of Elementary School Principals suggested educators do the following things to help their schools become more culturally responsive. Educators will:

- Conduct individual and building-wide self-assessments (i.e. Inter cultural Development Inventory).

- Create a positive climate and culture by intentionally promoting inclusivity and positive relations among students, among teachers and staff, and between students and adults on site.

- Explore innovative ways to reach the surrounding community, especially families, to utilize their strengths, keep them better informed, and involve them in creating and sustaining a positive climate and culture.

This section will explore teachers' beliefs and expectations, biases, microaggressions and culturally relevant interventions.

Can teachers' beliefs and expectations influence student success?

In *Nelson Beats the Odds*, Mr. Stevenson tells Nelson and Jeremy they aren't going to college. Instead of Mr. Stevenson's comments discouraging Nelson, they fueled him to accomplish his dream of going to college. Mr. Stevenson was representative of a teacher Ronnie Sidney, II, LCSW had when he was in eighth grade. Dr. Donna Ford, Professor of Education and Human Development at Vanderbilt University said, "When teachers understand how a student's background can affect his or her behavior in the classroom, they can build better relationships and diminish the effects that double stigma has on their students."

Implicit and explicit bias

Implicit bias is a comment or action that subtly and often unconsciously or unintentionally expresses a prejudiced attitude toward a member of a marginalized group (such as a racial minority). Implicit bias refers to a natural process by which we take information, and we judge people based on generalizations regarding that information. Unlike explicit bias (which reflects the attitudes or beliefs that one endorses at a conscious level), implicit bias is the bias in judgment and/or behavior that results from subtle cognitive processes (e.g., implicit attitudes and implicit stereotypes) that often operate at a level below conscious awareness and without intentional control.

Implicit biases about sex and race may influence how behaviors are perceived and how they are addressed. Personal and cultural beliefs shape our attitudes about students' challenging behaviors. Implicit bias drives suspensions of African-American students in the following ways:

- African-American children make up only 19% of preschool enrollment, but comprise 47% of preschoolers suspended one or more times.

- African-American boys are 4x more likely to be suspended than their white counterparts.

- African-American girls are suspended 12x more than girls any other race.

- High school graduation rates among African Americans with disabilities are 40 percentage points (43%) lower than national graduation rates (83%).

- African-American and Hispanics face much higher rates of school disciplinary actions, drop-out rates and experience lower rates of graduation.

Implicit and explicit bias disproportionately lead to preschool expulsions and suspensions of African American students, which undermine children's access to educational opportunities. Chronic Pre-K absenteeism is associated with both lower exit test scores, reading skills, cognitive skills, and social-emotional skills. Researcher Walter Gilliam used sophisticated eye-tracking technology to find out which group of students preschool teachers observe the closest. Findings revealed preschool teachers judge children's behavior differently based on race. When expecting challenging behaviors, pre-school teachers gazed longer at African-American children, especially African-American boys, than any other demographic.

Microaggressions

Derald Wing Sue, Ph.D., describes microaggressions as, "everyday verbal, nonverbal, and environmental slights, snubs, or insults, whether intentional or unintentional, which communicate hostile, derogatory, or negative messages to target persons based solely upon their marginalized group membership." Microaggressions are based on a person's race, disability, socioeconomic status, gender, sexual orientation, nationality or religion.

Policing the language, sleeping habits, clothing and hair of students are everyday micoaggressions teachers commit. Aaron Baker goes into greater detail in his article "3 racial microaggressions that teachers commit every day — and how to avoid them." Comments and behaviors around these topics often marginalize youth, particularly youth of color who don't feel like their culture is appreciated in the classroom.

Examples of microaggressions in the classroom

- Failing to learn to pronounce or continuing to mispronounce the names of students after they have corrected you.

- Scheduling tests and project due dates on religious or cultural holidays.

- Disregarding religious traditions or their details i.e. effect of fasting.

- Ignoring student-to-student microaggressions, even when the interaction is not course-related.

- Featuring pictures of students of only one ethnicity or gender on the school website.

- Having students engage in required reading where the protagonists are always white.

- Setting low expectations for students from particular groups, neighborhoods, or feeder patterns.

- Calling on, engaging and validating one gender, class, or race of students while ignoring other students during class.

- Anticipating students' emotional responses based on gender, sexual orientation, race or ethnicity.

- Using inappropriate humor in class that degrades students from different groups.

- Expressing racially charged political opinions in class assuming that the targets of those opinions do not exist in class.

- Using the term "illegals" to reference undocumented students.

- Singling students out or making them the spokesperson for their particular group.

- Denying the experiences of students by questioning the credibility and validity of their stories.

- Using sexist language or heteronormative metaphors.

What can educators do to decrease microaggressions and bias?

Educators will:

- Use interventions designed to address implicit biases.

- Provide extra training and support for staff.

- Respond to the person rather than reacting to their behaviors.

- Conduct a comparative analysis between the Core Standards and the population you are teaching.

- Set high expectations and reduce "deficient thinking" energy.

- Conduct morning "check-ins".

- Recognize that African-American males are different racially and socially.

- Maximize students' importance in the world.

- Use restorative justice approaches to discipline.

Discussion questions:

1. Write down as many identity descriptors as possible to help identify your cultural, philosophical, and social identity and begin to understand the social contexts that guide individual belief systems.

2. Recall an incident that occurred early in your life in which you felt different from people around you. What happened? How did you feel? How did this incident influence the choices you make as an educator?

3. Test your cultural sensitivity and diversity awareness by taking this personal inventory. After working with a student who represents a different race, ethnicity, gender, ability or sexual orientation, ask yourself the following questions::

    1. What was comfortable or uncomfortable?

    2. What was sensitive or insensitive?

    3. What was easy to address or difficult to address?

    4. Is there anything you wish to change about the encounter?

    5. What personal biases did the encounter make you aware of?

▲ The Westmoreland Children And Youth Association Wrote Essays After Reading The "Rest In Peace RaShawn" Script

Sources and other supplemental information

1. "Discretion and Disproportionality: Explaining the Underrepresentation of High-Achieving Students of Color in Gifted Programs" by Jason A. Grissom & Christopher Redding- http://journals.sagepub.com/doi/abs/10.1177/2332858415622175

2. "Teacher expectations reflect racial biases, Johns Hopkins study suggests" by Jill Rosen- https://hub.jhu.edu/2016/03/30/racial-bias-teacher-expectations-black-white/

3. "Why Can't We Just Get Along? Interpersonal Biases and Interracial Distrust" by John Dovidio, Samuel L. Gaertner, Kerry Kawakami, and Gordon Hodson- http://psychotherapy-and-psychoanalysis.com/NPI_articles_for_download/Dovidio_aversive_racism-2.pdf

4. "Do Early Educators' Implicit Biases Regarding Sex and Race Relate to Behavior Expectations and Recommendations of Preschool Expulsions and Suspensions?" by Walter S. Gilliam, PhD, Angela N. Maupin, PhD, Chin R. Reyes, PhD, Maria Accavitti, BS and Frederick Shic, PhD- https://medicine.yale.edu/childstudy/zigler/publications/Preschool%20Implicit%20Bias%20Policy%20Brief_final_9_26_276766_5379_v1.pdf

5. "Examples of Microaggressions in the Classroom"- https://www.messiah.edu/download/downloads/id/921/Microaggressions_in_the_Classroom.pdf

6. "His Teacher Told Him He Wouldn't Go To College, Then He Did" by Sophia Alvarez Boyd- https://www.npr.org/sections/ed/2017/04/23/520021794/his-teacher-told-him-he-wouldnt-go-to-college-then-he-did

Photo Credit: Kelsee Scott, Kelsee Scott Portraits LLC
Featured: Dr. Ronnie Sidney, Sr. and Ronnie Sidney, II, LCSW

TRAUMA

Tameka's New Dress and *Rest in Peace RaShawn* explore trauma in sensitive, kid-friendly ways. Tameka grows up in an impoverished, drug abusing home, and faces bullies at her new school. A neighborhood gang recruits Jeremy after he witnesses his brother's murder in *Rest in Peace RaShawn*. Tameka and Jeremy's experiences are similar to many of the students you interact with each day.

Nationally, 61% of children under 17 years-old were exposed to violence. Over half of all children attending school have been exposed to trauma. Teacher's risk re-traumatizing children who have experienced trauma by establishing rigid rules and consequences. Students with trauma histories are regularly subject to school discipline and exclusionary practices on a repeated basis. In this section, we will explore trauma, parental substance abuse, grand families, and trauma-informed schools.

What is trauma?

Traumas are frightening, often dangerous, and/or violent events or conditions that are experienced as overwhelming to a family and/or any or all its individual members. The four types of trauma are:

- Acute Trauma- A single event that lasts for a limited time.

- Chronic Trauma- The experience of multiple traumatic events, often over a long period of time.

- Complex Trauma- Multiple traumatic events (emotional abuse and neglect, sexual abuse, physical abuse, domestic violence) that begin during early childhood and occur within care giving system, which is a source of safety and stability.

- Historical & Racial Trauma- Collective and cumulative trauma experienced by a group across generations that are still suffering the effects and current experiences of race-based trauma (i.e. slavery, Jim Crow, Native American displacement and genocide).

Traumas can be stressful and impact individuals physically and mentally. Examples of traumas include:

- Accidents, natural disasters, illness, or injury.

- Fire, motor accidents, or cancer.

- Threat or harm to others.

- Death/suicide of loved one, witness to violence, or war.

- Threat or harm to self.
- Childhood sexual abuse, physical assault, robbery, rape, or combat trauma.

Trauma and the brain

- Brain scans of the prefrontal cortex, which is associated with executive functioning and planning, show less gray and white matter.
- The hippocampus, the region of the brain associated with learning, is noticeably smaller.
- The amygdala, which is responsible for our behavior and survival instincts, is increasingly activated.
- Traumatized children will often score lower on IQ test then their ability.
- Varying degrees of cognitive impairment and emotional dysregulation.
- Structuring and organizing information may be difficult for traumatized children due to delays in certain areas of the brain.

Trauma's impact on education and behavior

- Fight, flight, freeze and faint are adaptive stress responses that can have an adverse impact on children's behaviors.
- Difficulty with attention and focus, learning disabilities, low self-esteem, impaired socio-emotional development, and sleep disturbances.
- Increased risk of developing mental and behavioral health issues.
- Trauma can impact school performances (i.e. lower GPA, higher absence rate).
- Evidence suggests some children develop sensory processing difficulties which can contribute to problems with writing and reading.
- Students who have experienced trauma may be distrustful of teachers because authority figures have failed to provide safety for them in the past.

In *Tameka's New Dress*, the school guidance spoke with Tameka and she disclosed abuse and neglect. As an educator, you are a mandated reporter and required to report physical, sexual and emotional abuse and neglect. Reports of abuse and neglect should be made to your local social services department or the Child Abuse and Neglect Hotline at 1-800-552-7096. Reports can be made anonymously, however, you can leave your name and contact information. The list below is a tool you can use to recognize signs of child abuse and neglect.

Recognizing child abuse and neglect

Physical Abuse

- Physical Indicators
    - Unexplained bruises or burns on face, torso, back, buttocks, thighs
    - Multiple injuries in various stages of healing
    - Bruises/welts resembling instruments used i.e. belt, cord
    - Injuries regularly appearing after absence, weekend, etc.
- Behavioral Indicators
    - Reports injury by caretaker
    - Uncomfortable with physical contact
    - Complains of soreness or moves uncomfortably
    - Wears clothing inappropriate to weather (to cover body)
    - Afraid to go home
    - Behavioral extremes (withdraw, aggressive)
    - Apprehensive when other children cry

Physical Neglect

- Physical Indicators
    - Consistent hunger, poor hygiene
    - Unattended physical problems or medical needs

- ◇ Consistent lack of supervision
- ◇ Abandonment
- Behavioral Indicators
  - ◇ Reports no caretaker at home
  - ◇ Begs, hordes food
  - ◇ Frequently absent or tardy
  - ◇ Constant fatigue, listlessness, or falling asleep in class
  - ◇ Extended stays in school i.e. early arrival and late departure

Sexual Abuse

- Physical Indicators
  - ◇ Sexually Transmitted Infection i.e. pre-teens
  - ◇ Pregnancy
  - ◇ Difficulty walking or sitting
  - ◇ Pain or itching in genital area
  - ◇ Torn, stained, or bloody underclothing
  - ◇ Bruises/bleeding in external genitalia
- Behavioral Indicators
  - ◇ Reports sexual abuse
  - ◇ Highly sexualized play
  - ◇ Detailed, age inappropriate understanding of sexual behavior
  - ◇ Role reversal, overly concerned for siblings
  - ◇ Exhibits delinquent behavior
  - ◇ May attempt suicide or other self-injurious behavior
  - ◇ Deterioration in academic performance

Trauma Informed Schools

A program, organization, or system that is trauma-informed:

- Realizes the widespread impact of trauma in schools and understands potential paths for recovery.

- Recognizes the signs and symptoms of trauma in students, families, staff, and others involved with the school system.

- Responds by fully integrating knowledge about trauma into school policies, procedures, and practices.

- Seeks to actively resist re-traumatization.

Classroom elements to avoid

Educators will avoid:

- Stressful and anxious environments with little to no support.

- Teaching to the "bell-shaped curve" because it often marginalizes traumatized children.

- Serious atmospheres absent of fun and enjoyment.

- A lack of classroom supervision or too much unsupervised communication among peers.

- Negative teacher expectations and criticism.

- Rigid, constricting learning environments.

- Unpredictable learning environments that can be easily disrupted.

- Competitive classroom environments that set children up for failure and disappointment.

Six ways to become a trauma-informed school by the National Resilience Institute

- Education- Provide staff development for educators on trauma's impact on learning.

- Safety- Help students feel safe physically, socially, emotionally and academically.

- Holistic- Meet students' needs by taking into account their relationships, self-regulation, academic competence, and physical and emotional well-being.

- Community- Connect students to the school community and provide them with multiple opportunities to practice newly developing skills.

- Accountability- Embrace a shared responsibility for all students.

- Adaptability- Staff anticipate and adapt to the ever-changing needs of students.

Ten tips for managing escalating behaviors at school

As an educator, you may encounter students with trauma histories who become agitated- this can be very challenging and anxiety producing. Students often warn us before their behavior escalates and it is important we intervene before it's too late. By following the tips listed below, you may be able to redirect students before their behavior escalates.

1. Be empathetic- Try not to judge or discount others feelings.

2. Clarify messages- Listen for the students' real message; what is the reality of their distress.

3. Respect personal space- Stand at least 1.5 to 3 feet from a student whose behaviors are escalating.

4. Be aware of your body position- Standing eye-to-eye or toe-to-toe with a dysregulated student sends a threatening messages.

5. Ignore challenging questions- When a student challenges your authority, redirect the individual's attention and avoid power struggles.

6. Permit verbal venting if safely possible- Allow a student to release as much energy as possible by venting verbally.

7. Set and enforce reasonable limits- If the student becomes belligerent, defensive, or disruptive, state limits clearly and offer choices and consequences.

8. Keep your nonverbal cues nonthreatening- The more control students' lose, the less attention they are paying to your actual words.

9. Avoid overreacting- Remain rational, calm and professional.

10. Use physical techniques and school resource officers only as a last resort- use the least restrictive method of intervention possible.

Discussion questions

1. How aware do you think school staff are about the types of trauma students' experience?

2. How can you support youth who have experienced trauma?

3. What types of trauma did Tameka and Jeremy experience in their respective stories?

Sources and other supplemental information

1. The National Child Traumatic Stress Network- https://www.nctsn.org/

2. Substance Abuse and Mental Health Services Administration- https://www.samhsa.gov/nctic/trauma-interventions

3. "Paradise Lost: The Neurobiological and Clinical Consequences of Child Abuse and Neglect" by Charles B Nemeroff- https://www.ncbi.nlm.nih.gov/pubmed/26938439

4. "Unlocking the Door to Learning: Trauma-Informed Classrooms & Transformational Schools" by Maura McInerney, Esq. and Amy McKlindon, M.S.W.- https://www.elc-pa.org/wp-content/uploads/2015/06/Trauma-Informed-in-Schools-Classrooms-FINAL-December2014-2.pdf

5. Virginia Department of Social Services- http://www.dss.virginia.gov/

6. "The Principal's Guide to Building Culturally Responsive Schools" by The National Association of Elementary School Principals- https://www.naesp.org/sites/default/files/NAESP_Culturally_Responsive_Schools_Guide.pdf

GRIEF AND LOSS

Tameka's New Dress and *Rest in Peace RaShawn Reloaded* explore grief and loss. In *Tameka's New Dress*, Tameka experiences the loss of her biological father and mother. In *Rest in Peace RaShawn Reloaded*, Jeremy's older brother RaShawn is shot and killed by a police officer. In this section we will explore grief and loss and share ways educators can support their students.

What is grief?

Grief is a natural response to losing someone or something that is important to you. Individuals may feel a variety of emotions, like sadness or loneliness. The reflection of a connection that has been lost can be very difficult for young people. Students may experience grief after the:

- Loss of a loved one.
- Loss of a relationship.
- Family moves to a new area.
- Divorce of family members.
- Diagnosis of a medical illness i.e. chronic, life-threatening.
- Development of a physical or intellectual disability.
- Change of teachers.

Students who experience grief and loss may exhibit regressive, childlike behaviors. Younger children may experience separation anxiety when away from their parent. Expect questions about grief due to their inability to comprehend the permanence of death. Teenagers may get angry more often, have difficulty concentrating at school, and become emotionally distant. Sleep onset and maintenance issues are common for teenagers who are experiencing grief.

Stages of grief

The Kubler-Ross model by Elisabeth Kubler Ross and David Kessler divides grief into five stages and helps us frame and identify what individuals may be feeling. The five stages of grief include the following:

- Denial: When you first learn of a loss, it is normal to think, "This isn't happening." You may feel shocked or numb. This is a temporary way to deal with the rush of overwhelming emotion. It is a defense mechanism.

- Anger: As reality sets in, you face the pain of your loss. You may feel frustrated and helpless. These feelings later turn into anger. You might direct it toward other people, a higher power, or life in general. To be angry with a loved one who died and left you alone is natural, too.

- Bargaining: During this stage, you dwell on what you could have done to prevent the loss. Common thoughts are "If only…" and "What if…" You may also try to strike a deal with a higher power.

- Depression: Sadness sets in as you begin to understand the loss and its effect on your life. Signs of depression include crying, sleep issues, and a decreased appetite. You may feel overwhelmed, regretful, and lonely.

- Acceptance: In this final stage of grief, you accept the reality of your loss can't be changed. Although you still feel sad, you are able to start moving forward with your life.

Ways to support someone who is experiencing grief and loss

Grief is a natural process that often runs its course without clinical treatment, however, it can also be complicated for those who are unable to accept loss and adjust to life circumstances. Prolonged, complicated grief may extend beyond six months and preoccupy the thoughts of a loved one. Suicidal ideation, insomnia, hallucinations, and declined cognitive functioning are symptoms of complicated grief.

It is important that educators seek out ways to provide reassurance for students so they do not feel like they are alone. Educators can help better support students who are experiencing grief and loss by:

- Understanding you are not expected to solve the problem.

- Learning to listen, provide support, and reassurance.

- Remembering the grief process is personalized and often lasts longer than expected.

- Being patient with the grieving person.

- Being empathic and non-judgmental while listening to students retell their story multiple times.

- Learning from the person who is grieving.

- Not assuming you know what the person is feeling and experiencing.

Expressions of grief

Students may experience:

- Sadness, crying, and depression.

- Irritability, sleep problems, anxiety, and fear.

- Anger, sadness, guilt, despair, relief and depression.

- Loss of appetite, loss of motivation and loss of concentration/focus.

Contact the guidance counselor if you observe a significant change in the following behaviors:

- Change in eating habits.
- Lower academic productivity.
- Withdrawal from social activities.
- Increase in complaints of pain or illness.
- Changes in personality.
- Responds to staff and students who talk about the person who died inappropriately.
- Acting in ways that are unusual for him/her.

Spirituality and grief

In *Rest in Peace RaShawn Reloaded*, a minister presided over the funeral of RaShawn and provided the family with reassurance. The comic uses spirituality as a tool to help Jeremy process grief. It is important to be aware of the spiritual reactions students may have regarding grief. The following examples explain how individuals process grief and loss spiritually:

- *Buddhism*- there are special meditations that Buddhists often use at the time of death and they may ask to limit sedation of their dying loved one so that he or she can maintain consciousness for the meditation.
- *Christianity*- mourners take comfort in the idea that their loved one has ascended to the Kingdom of Heaven, to be reunited with other deceased loves ones and to be with God.
- *Hinduism*- family typically washes the body in a special ritual to prepare it for cremation on the day of death; belief in eternal life through reincarnation.
- *Judaism*- burials typically take place within a day or two of death; forgiveness is an important part of the grieving process.
- *Islam*- death is often seen as the return to the creator, Allah, who will judge the soul based on how life was lived; burial is custom and cremation is forbidden.

What should I say to a student who is experiencing grief?

One of the biggest challenges for educators is knowing what to say to someone who is experiencing grief and loss. Actively resisting re-traumatization means we must be conscious of what we say or do to a student who is experiencing grief and loss. Below is a list of suggestions of what to say and what not to say to individuals experiencing grief:

Say:

- I am so sorry.
- I wish I had the right words, just know that I care.
- I don't know how you feel, but I am here to help in any way that I can.
- You will be in my thoughts.
- We all need help at times like this and I am here for you.
- Nothing and just be with the person and listen.

Do not say:

- At least he/she lived a long life, many people die young.
- He/she is in a better place.
- He/she brought this on.
- There is a reason for everything.
- It's been a while now, aren't you feeling better yet?
- He/she was such a good person that God wanted him/her.
- You think your loss was bad, I lost someone even younger.
- It was his/her time to go.
- Everyone dies some day.
- Be strong.
- I know how you feel.

Discussion questions:

1. How did the main characters in *Rest in Peace RaShawn* and *Tameka's New Dress* cope with grief and loss?
2. As an educator, how should you address grief and loss in the classroom?

Sources and other supplemental information

1. Five stages of grief- https://grief.com/the-five-stages-of-grief/
2. Coalition to support grieving students- https://grievingstudents.org
3. "Grief & Loss in Individuals with ID/DD" by Mojgan Pourmand, Psy.D.

BULLYING

Throughout *Tameka's New Dress,* Tameka faced a variety of challenges. Her most difficult challenge is standing up the school bully Mesha. The conflict between Tameka and Mesha introduces readers to the troubling concept of colorism. Mesha persecuted Tameka for being a fair-complexioned, Black girl with 'good hair'. Instead of Tameka confronting Mesha violently, she used assertive communication to deescalate the situation. In this section, we will explore bullying and ways educators can increase awareness about bullying in their schools.

What is bullying?

Aggressive behaviors that include an imbalance of power and repetition are strong indicators of bullying. Bullies use this power to control or harm their victims. The behaviors bullies' exhibit have the potential to happen more than once.

Bullying is classified in three types: verbal bullying, relational bullying, and physical bullying. Examples of verbal bullying includes, but is not limited to the following:

- Name-calling
- Teasing
- Inappropriate sexual comments
- Threating to cause harm
- Relational bullying, sometimes referred to as social bullying, involves hurting someone's relationship or reputation

Relational bullying impacts people interpersonally. It includes the following:

- Spreading nasty rumors about someone.
- Shaming a person on social media (i.e. cyberbullying).
- Leaving someone out of a group on purpose.
- Embarrassing a person in public.
- Telling other not be friends with someone.

Physical bullying involves hurting a person's possessions or their physical body. Physical bullying includes the following:

- Breaking or taking someone's possession.
- Punching/kicking/pinching someone.
- Spitting on someone.
- Tripping/Pushing someone.
- Making inappropriate hand gestures.

Bullying can occur before school, during school and after school. Most reported bullying occurs in the school building, however, a significant percentage occurs on the school bus or playground. Social media and students' neighborhoods are common places where bullying occurs.

Increasing awareness about bullying

Educators can:

- Develop a formal anti-bullying program or incorporate anti-bullying lessons and activities into a curriculum.
- Use the internet or library to research bullying prevention strategies.
- Create cyberbullying presentations that include role-play and conflict resolution strategies.
- Plan classroom meetings or professional development workshops about bullying prevention strategies.
- Use creative writing to speak out against bullying and find ways to teach bystanders how to help.
- Encourage students to use their creativity to develop skits and artwork that address the effects of bullying.
- Lead classroom discussions that give students an opportunity to openly talk about bullying.

Discussion questions

1. If a child is being bullied in school, who should you contact?

    a. Child's parent

    b. School principal

    c. School counselor

    d. All of the above

2. Contact the National Suicide Prevention Lifeline online or at 1-800-273-TALK (8255) if the student is experiencing the following emotions or thoughts.

    a. Hopelessness

    b. Helplessness

    c. Thoughts of suicide

    d. All of the above

3. Call 911 if there has been a crime or someone is at immediate risk of harm. True or False?

4. How would you rate the way your school or district addresses bullying? 1 being poor and 10 being fantastic. How could your school or district better address bullying?

Sources and other supplemental Information

1. Stop Bullying- https://www.stopbullying.gov/

GANGS

Community violence and gangs are explored in *Rest in Peace RaShawn*. The Sauce Street Gang terrorizes Jeremy's neighborhood and makes it difficult for him to navigate his way to school. Lil' G is the leader of a fictional street gang called the Sauce Street Gang. He threatens to kill Jeremy after Jeremy disrespects him in front of the other gang members. The loss of Jeremy's older brother RaShawn left a void that Lil' G attempted to fill. Lil' G used Jeremy's anger, vengeance and vulnerability as a tool to wreak havoc on Habib's store.

Many of the students walking through the halls of your school feel the impact of gang violence. One of the risk factors for youth joining gangs is early academic failure and lack of school attachment. This section includes information about gangs and strategies educators can use to address the issue.

Gangs like the Bloods, Crips, Pirus, Black Disciples, Sureños and MS-13 operate in communities all over the country. Here are some warning signs your students may be in a gang:

- Declining school attendance or performance.

- Withdraws from preferred activities, family and friends.

- Admits to "hanging out" with kids in gangs.

- Shows an unusual interest in one or two particular colors of clothing or a particular logo.

- Has an unusual interest in gang-influenced music, videos, movies, or websites.

- Uses unusual slang, handshakes and intricate hand signs to communicate with friends.

- Has specific drawings or gang symbols on school books, clothes, walls, or displays tattoos.

- Unexplained physical injuries from fights.
- Has unexplained cash or expensive clothing/jewelry.
- Stays out late without reason.

Five reasons why young people join gangs

The Los Angeles Police Department identified five reasons why young people join gangs. Their motivations usually fall within one of the following:

1. Identity or Recognition - Being part of a gang allows the gang member to achieve a level of status he/she feels impossible outside the gang culture.

2. Protection - many members join because they live in the gang area and are, therefore, subject to violence by rival gangs. Joining guarantees support in case of attack and retaliation for transgressions.

3. Fellowship and Brotherhood - To the majority of gang members, the gang functions as an extension of the family and may provide companionship lacking in the gang member's home environment. Many older brothers and relatives belong, or have belonged to the gang.

4. Intimidation - Some members are forced to join if their membership will contribute to the gang's criminal activity. Some join to intimidate others in the community not involved in gang activity.

5. Criminal Activity - Some join a gang to engage in narcotics activity and benefit from the group's profits and protection.

What can educators do to prevent gang involvement?

Educators can:

- Gain more knowledge on the subject.
- Provide information and support to parents.
- Implement awareness programs.
- Be a positive role model and set the right example.
- Encourage good study habits.
- Teach young people how to cope with peer pressure.
- Encourage young people to participate in positive after school activities with adult supervision.
- Talk to young people about the dangers and consequences of gang involvement. Let the young person know you do not want to see them hurt or arrested.

- Collaborate and network with community resources.

Discussion questions

1. What is your strategy to combat gang influence at your school?

Sources and other supplemental Information

1. Los Angeles Police Department- http://www.lapdonline.org/get_informed/content_basic_view/23473

SELF-CARE

Educators are often under-resourced, over-tasked and at times, under-appreciated. More than many other occupations, educators need to take care of themselves. Doing so is incredibly beneficial, for family members and students, especially when it comes to supporting students affected by trauma, poverty, and disabilities. Teaching is emotional labor, so here are some ways for trauma-informed educators to avoid burnout, cope with stress and care for themselves. In this section we will explore burnout, compassion fatigue, and self-care tips.

12 stages of burnout

Stage 1: Compulsion to prove oneself, excessive ambition.

Stage 2: Push to work harder.

Stage 3: Neglecting personal needs.

State 4: Displacement of conflict.

Stage 5: Revision of value system, self-worth based on job.

Stage 6: Denial of problems, believe that others are lazy.

Stage 7: Withdrawal from social situations.

Stage 8: Obvious behavioral change noticed by others.

Stage 9: Loss of contact with self.

Stage 10: Inner emptiness sets in.

Stage 11: Depression sets in.

Stage 12: Burnout syndrome (mental or physical collapse).

Compassion fatigue

Dr. Charles Figley defined compassion fatigue as "an extreme state of tension and preoccupation with the suffering of those being helped to the degree that it can create a secondary traumatic stress for the helper." Compassion fatigue is prevalent amongst educators, social workers and healthcare professionals; it's a common result of working with individuals who have endured traumatic experiences.

Compassion fatigue affects a personal cognitively, behaviorally, emotionally, spiritually and somatically. It can cause lowered concentration, irritability, withdrawal, anxiety, depression, loss of faith, sweating, body aches, sleep problems and more.

The 5 Phases of Compassion Fatigue

1. Zealot: Motivated by idealism and ready to serve and problem solve; energetic and eager.

2. Irritability: Begins to cut corners, avoid student/parent contact, mock peers and students; distancing.

3. Withdrawal: Loses patience with students, becomes defensive, neglects self and others, is chronically fatigued, loses hope, views self as a victim and isolates self.

4. Zombie: Views others as incompetent or ignorant; loses patience and humor; easily upset.

5. Pathology and victimization or maturation and renewal:

    ◊ In this phase, the educator can choose pathology and victimization or maturation and renewal.

    ◊ Pathology and victimization result when no action is taken (may leave the profession).

    ◊ Maturation and renewal are possible only when the educator acknowledges the symptoms of compassion fatigue and takes direct action to overcome it (resiliency).

Self-care tips

- The need in the education field will always be greater than the resources available.

- The suffering of others is not yours.

- Look at how you measure "success" for yourself, students, and your colleagues.

- Remember to care for yourself, you are the instrument to help others.

- Value small changes in students.

- Don't take your students' issues home with you.

30 Self-care activities for educators

1. Meal preparation

2. Take lunch breaks

3. Eat your favorite comfort food

4. Drink water

5. Make time for relaxation
6. 8-10 hours of sleep
7. Meditation
8. Yoga
9. Stretching
10. Follow 80/20 rule at home
11. Make fun a priority
12. Socialize regularly
13. Go for a walk at lunchtime
14. Take your dog for a walk after work
15. Use your sick leave
16. Listen to your favorite song on repeat
17. Get some exercise before/after work regularly
18. Keep a reflective journal
19. Use your creativity
20. Seek and engage in regular supervision or consultation
21. Engage with a non-work hobby
22. Make time to engage with positive friends and family
23. Write three good things you did each day
24. Have a glass of wine with colleagues after work
25. Go to the movies or do something else you enjoy
26. Talk to you friend about how you are coping with work and life demands
27. Engage in regular supervision or consulting with a more experienced colleague
28. Set healthy boundaries between students, colleagues and family members
29. Read professional journals
30. Attend professional development programs

Discussion question

Creating a self-care plan will require you to focus on how you take care of yourself physically, emotionally and cognitively. Ask yourself the following questions:

1. List five things you will do to take care of your body in a healthy way.

2. List five things you will do to take care of your feelings in a healthy way.

3. List five things you will do to improve your mind and understand yourself better.

Checklist for Resiliency

Answer the following questions.

1. What are my strengths?

2. What has helped me endure previous difficult times?

3. What healthy things can I do to soothe myself when I'm faced with uncertainty?

4. Is there something I can do to influence what will happen next? If so, what?

5. What are my resources to increase my resilience?

6. How can I ask for what I need?

Sources and other supplemental information

1. "Why it's so hard for teachers to take care of themselves (and 4 ways to start) by Jennifer Gonzalez- https://www.cultofpedagogy.com/teacher-self-care/

NELSON BEATS THE ODDS SERIES
STRESS REDUCTION KIT
Take these steps to reduce your stress and move on.

1. Place kit on FIRM surface.

2. Follow directions in circle of kit.

3. Repeat step 2 as necessary, or until unconscious.

4. If unconscious, cease stress reduction activity.

STUDENT ACTIVITIES

Nelson Beats the Odds Comic Creator App

Author-therapist Ronnie Sidney, II, LCSW's latest addition to his box of therapeutic tools is the Nelson Beats The Odds Comic Creator app for iOS mobile devices. The free self-esteem app allows iPhone, iPod and iPad users to substitute their own photos to create composite images personalizing the characters' faces in the book's illustrations. The author-therapist collaborated with Potenza Global Solutions, a successful IT company out of India, and released the app on October 7, 2015.

Nelson Beats The Odds Comic Creator is a simple way to inspire the world with creative photos. Users can snap a photo with their iOS device or choose a photo from their photo library. The companion app allows users to apply stunning filters, photo effects, and an ever-growing collection of stickers, comic strips, frames, word bubbles, text art and more. The self-esteem app includes one more big surprise, free access to *Nelson Beats the Odds* and *Tameka's New Dress* eBooks.

What does the Nelson Beats the Odds Comic Creator App do?

eBooks

Read Amazon best-seller *Nelson Beats the Odds* or *Tameka's New Dress* for free.

Photo editing

Improve photos with creative tools to change brightness, contrast and saturation. Resize, zoom or rotate the photo as well.

Photo cropping

Crop the face out of your favorite photo and place it on the body of your favorite *Nelson Beats The Odds* character. Choose from 8 fun photo frames.

Stickers

Choose from an assortment of exciting character stickers, hairstyles, mustaches, clothing, glasses, sports, text art and emoji's.

Comic strip

Add up to five photos and choose from our great selection of frames.

Photo filters

Apply one of our 14 spectacular photo filters - with more on the way.

Nelson Beats the Odds Comic Creator Activities

1. *Read Nelson Beats the Odds* and *Tameka's New Dress* eBook by selecting Get Books Now. Press Get Books Now and select which book you want to read. Look through the workbook and complete the *Nelson Beats the Odds* and *Tameka's New Dress* activities.

2. Select Photo Library and select a photo from your library. Add text, stickers, frames and captions to make your photo look more creative.

3. Choose a photo under Photo Fun, take a selfie and crop your face onto the photo.

4. Select Photo Memes and take a selfie or choose a picture from your photo library. Add one of our three filters to your photo.

5. Select Comic Strip and select the photos you would like to use to create your very own comic.

6. With your parents' permission, share your photos on social media using the hashtags #nelsonbeatstheodds #NBTO #iBeatTheOdds.

Photo Credit: Ronnie Sidney, II, LCSW
Featured: Hervé Tullet

NELSON BEATS THE ODDS SERIES
HOW TO TASTE A BOOK

Sometimes it can be difficult to choose a book to read. Here is a list of steps you can take to choose the right book for you.
Directions: Circle the book or your choice, then complete questions 2-4. Don't forget to complete the critique below.

1 **Pick a book.** Choose up to three books for comparison.

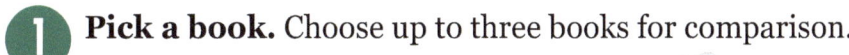

2 **Look at front cover.** Closely review the artwork on the front cover. What's the main subject? What's in the background? Imagine what the book is about.

 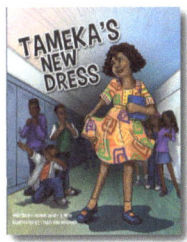 

3 **Read the back and inside flap.** This is where you find the book's summary along with information about the author/illustrator.

4 **Read the book.** Read the first 10 pages before deciding. If you got this far, you should give the book a chance. It sometimes takes a while to get into the author's voice.

What I like	What I don't like	
		Tell my friends 😊
		It's fine 😐
		Not for me ☹

NAME:	DATE:	BOOK READ:

Reading Level: Grade Five

Reading Level: Grade Five

NELSON BEATS THE ODDS SERIES
SOMEBODY WANTED BUT SO THEN

Directions: After reading a book from the Nelson Beats The Odds Series, use the parses below to answer the question. Next, write a short summery of the book on the following page.

SOMEBODY → Who is the main character in this book?

WANTED → What did the character want to do or happen?

BUT → What is the problem in the story?

SO → How did the character try to solve the problem?

THEN → What was the resolution? How did the story end?

NAME: DATE: BOOK READ:

NELSON BEATS THE ODDS SERIES
SOMEBODY WANTED BUT SO THEN

NELSON BEATS THE ODDS SERIES

NAME:　　　　　DATE:　　　　　BOOK READ:

Reading Level: Grade Five

NELSON BEATS THE ODDS SERIES
MATCHING ACTIVITY

Directions: Match the words on the right with their definitions on the left.

Self-Publishing	1	A	The view that everyone deserves equal economic, political and social rights and opportunities.
Headmaster	2	B	Not interested; indifferent.
Attention-Deficit/Hyper-Activity Disorder (ADHD)	3	C	A disorder characterized by difficulty in understanding or using spoken or written language.
Potential	4	D	A condition giving rise to difficulties in acquiring knowledge and skills to the level expected of those of the same age.
Autism	5	E	To make a humming, buzzing, or hissing sound, as an object passing swiftly through the air.
Down Syndrome	6	F	Education that is modified for those with singular needs.
Dyslexia	7	G	A genetic disorder characterized by mild to severe mental impairment, weak muscle tone, shorter stature, and a flattened facial profile.
Whizzed	8	H	A disorder of children, characterized by impaired communication, rigidity, and emotional detachment.
Learning Disability	9	I	Publication of any book without the involvement of an established publisher. The author is in control.
Special Education	10	J	A condition, usually in children, characterized by inattention, hyperactivity, and impulsiveness.
Trauma	11	K	A condition that causes trouble with written expression.
Dysgraphia	12	L	Frightening or violent events that are experienced as overwhelming.
Social Justice	13	M	The person in charge of a private school.
Disinterested	14	N	Capable of being or becoming.

Answers: 1-I, 2-M, 3-J, 4-N, 5-H, 6-G, 7-C, 8-E, 9-D, 10-F, 11-L, 12-K, 13-A, 14-B

NAME:	DATE:	BOOK READ:

NELSON BEATS THE ODDS SERIES
CHARACTERS ON A ROLL

Directions: Gather a pair of dice and roll them. Answer the question that corresponds to the number on the dice.

Reading Level: Grade Five

2 Where will the main character be 20 years from now?

3 How does the main character change during the story?

4 OR What did the main character do to make you dislike him/her?

5 OR How is the role of the supporting character(s) important to the story?

6 OR Cite a phrase that helps the reader learn about the main character.

7 OR What are the main character's strengths? Weaknesses?

8 OR OR What will happen to the main character in the sequel to the book?

9 OR How does the main character interact with other characters?

10 OR Compare two characters. How are they alike? Different?

11 Why would you want to be or not be the main character's friend?

12 What inspired you about the main character?

NAME: DATE: BOOK READ:

Reading Level: Grade Five

NELSON BEATS THE ODDS SERIES
CHARACTER PROFILE

Directions: After reading "Tameka's New Dress", "Nelson Beats the Odds", or "Rest in Peace RaShawn".
Select two of your favorite characters from the book and answer the following questions.

Character 1

| 1 | Book Read | Character Name | Character Gender |

What does your character do to show their personality?
_____
_____

What does your character look like on the outside?
_____
_____

What does your character say to show their personality?
_____
_____

How does your character change, or what lesson does your character learn?
_____
_____

Character 2

| 2 | Book Read | Character Name | Character Gender |

What does your character do to show their personality?
_____
_____

What does your character look like on the outside?
_____
_____

What does your character say to show their personality?
_____
_____

How does your character change, or what lesson does your character learn?
_____
_____

| NAME: | DATE: | BOOK READ: |

Download @ www.creative-medicine.com   ©2018 Creative Medicine

Reading Level: Grade Five

NELSON BEATS THE ODDS SERIES
WORD SEARCH

Directions: Find and circle all of the following words. They may be horizontally, vertically, or diagonal.

```
H R D N P D O L D F F J C A I
H B U L L Y I N G Y R W T Q M
S V K A X Y H D O T I Y E W E
A S P J F F I T A M E K A T P
G D J S S A U R D U N A M P R
Q A J T D M H A D X D B W N A
C D V E E I S U J O S C O P S
L S R R K L S M N G C D R T H
J E R E M Y G A I L H P K S A
P R V O S J L C B R O H D E W
F B Z T K S S P G I O D O U N
W I P Y D U V I A H L E R S J
K H O P E F J C C O M I C S T
X G N E L S O N G J A W T I D
T K S I X C O M M U N I T Y M
```

DISABILITY   RASHAWN   FAMILY
TRAUMA   BULLYING   COMMUNITY
TAMEKA   SCHOOL   TEAMWORK
NELSON   DRESS   STEREOTYPE
JEREMY   COMICS
HOPE   FRIENDS

NAME: DATE: BOOK READ:

Reading Level: Grade Five

NELSON BEATS THE ODDS SERIES
WHAT I THINK ABOUT A BOOK

Directions: After reading "Tameka's New Dress", "Nelson Beats the Odds", or "Rest in Peace RaShawn", answer the following questions based on the book you selected. There are no wrong answers.

1. My favorite part..._____
2. This book reminded me of..._____
3. I predict that..._____
4. I wonder why..._____
5. My favorite character is..._____
6. I was confused when..._____
7. After reading, I felt..._____
8. I was surprised when..._____
9. A part that disappointed me was..._____
10. I pictured in my head..._____
11. I like this author because..._____
12. The ending was..._____
13. The theme is..._____
14. Some evidence is..._____
15. Some words I'm not sure of are..._____

| NAME: | DATE: | BOOK READ: |

Download @ www.creative-medicine.com   62   ©2018 Creative Medicine

NELSON BEATS THE ODDS SERIES
ACTION POSTER

Directions: Read "Tameka's New Dress", "Nelson Beats the Odds", or "Rest in Peace RaShawn".

Create a poster that helps promote or enlighten a topic from the book.

EXAMPLES

Nelson Beats the Odds- Learning disabilities, ADHD, stigma, friendship, and resilience.

Rest in Peace RaShawn Reloaded- Gangs, police involved shootings, mental health, grief, and social justice.

Tameka's New Dress- Abuse, bullying, family, substance abuse, conflict resolution, and colorism.

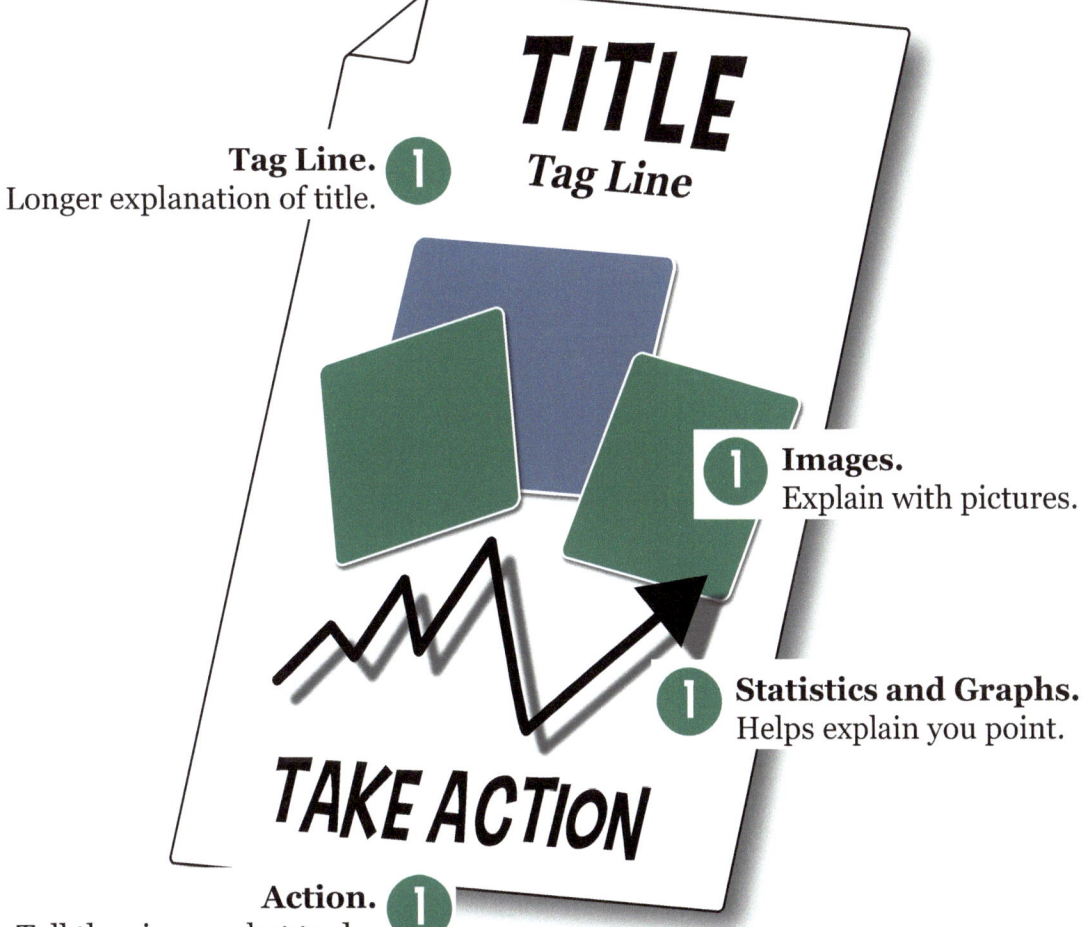

1 Clear Bold Title. It should be simple and clear.

Tag Line. 1 Longer explanation of title.

1 Images. Explain with pictures.

1 Statistics and Graphs. Helps explain you point.

Action. 1 Tell the viewer what to do.

NAME: DATE: BOOK READ:

BOOK LIST

1. Learning Disabilities and Related Disabilities: Strategies for Success by Janet W. Lerner and Beverley Johns

2. Promoting Racial Literacy in Schools: Differences That Make a Difference by Howard C. Stevenson

3. For White Folks Who Teach in the Hood… and the Rest of Y'all Too: Reality Pedagogy and Urban Education (Race, Education, and Democracy) by Christopher Emdin

4. More Than a Score: The New Uprising Against High-Stakes Testing by Jesse Hagopian and Diane Ravitch

5. The Body Keeps the Score: Brain, Mind, and Body in the Healing of Trauma by Bessel van der Kolk M.D.

6. Reaching & Teaching Children Exposed to Trauma by Barbara Sorrels

7. The Boy Who Was Raised as a Dog: And Other Stories from a Child Psychiatrist's Notebook--What Traumatized Children Can Teach Us About Loss, Love, and Healing by Bruce D. Perry and Maia Szalavitz

8. "Multiplication Is for White People": Raising Expectations for Other People's Children by Lisa Delpit

9. Why Are All the Black Kids Sitting Together in the Cafeteria?: And Other Conversations About Race by Beverly Daniel Tatum

10. Other People's Children: Cultural Conflict in the Classroom by Lisa Delpit

11. Lost at School: Why Our Kids with Behavioral Challenges are Falling Through the Cracks and How We Can Help Them by Ross W. Greene Ph.D.

12. Fostering Resilient Learners: Strategies for Creating a Trauma-Sensitive Classroom by Kristin Souers and Pete Hall

13. Better Than Carrots or Sticks: Restorative Practices for Positive Classroom Management by Dominique Smith and Douglas Fisher

14. Trauma-Sensitive Schools: Learning Communities Transforming Children's Lives, K–5 by Susan E. Craig and Jane Ellen Stevens

15. The Little Book of Restorative Discipline for Schools: Teaching Responsibility; Creating Caring Climates (The Little Books of Justice and Peacebuilding Series) by Lorraine Stutzman Amstutz and Judy H. Mullet

16. Pushout: The Criminalization of Black Girls in Schools by Monique Morris and Mankaprr Conteh

17. Between the World and Me by Ta-Nehisi Coates

18. The New Jim Crow: Mass Incarceration in the Age of Colorblindness by Michelle Alexander and Cornel West

19. Rest in Power: The Enduring Life of Trayvon Martin by Sybrina Fulton and Tracy Martin

20. The Hate U Give by Angie Thomas

21. All American Boys by Jason Reynolds and Brendan Keily

22. Tyler Johnson Was Here by Jay Coles

23. Dear Martin by Nic Stone

24. I Am Alfonso Jones Written by Tony Medina and Illustrated by John Jennings and Stacey Robinson

25. Ghost Boys by Jewell Parker Rhodes

26. How It Went Down by Kekla Magoon

27. They Can't Kill Us All by Wesley Lowery

28. Countering the Conspiracy to Destroy Black Boys by Jawanza Kunjufu

29. Overcoming Dyslexia: A New and Complete Science-Based Program for Reading Problems at Any Level by Sally Shaywitz M.D.

30. Driven to Distraction (Revised): Recognizing and Coping with Attention Deficit Disorder from Childhood Through Adulthood by Edward M. Hallowell M.D.

Ronnie Sidney II, LCSW's Bibliography

Nelson Beats The Odds (2015)

Tameka's New Dress (Nelson Beats The Odds) (Volume 2) (2016)

Nelson Beats The Odds: Compendium One (2016)

Rest in Peace RaShawn (Nelson Beats the Odds) (Volume 3) (2017)

Rest in Peace RaShawn Reloaded (Nelson Beats the Odds) (Volume 4) (2017)

African Americans Who Received Special Education Services and Succeeded Beyond Expectations: "Insecurities of Special Education: What It's Like to Be Black, Male, and Learning Disabled" (2018)

ADDITIONAL RESOURCES

Trauma

SAMHSA (https://www.samhsa.gov/)

The Substance Abuse and Mental Health Services Administration (SAMHSA) is the agency within the U.S. Department of Health and Human Services that leads public health efforts to advance the behavioral health of the nation. SAMHSA's mission is to reduce the impact of substance abuse and mental illness on America's communities.

NCTSN (https://www.nctsn.org/)

The National Child Traumatic Stress Network (NCTSN) was created to raise the standard of care and increase access to services for children and families who experience or witness traumatic events.

Sesame Street in Communities (https://sesamestreetincommunities.org/topics/traumatic-experiences/)

When a child endures a traumatic experience, the whole family feels the impact. But adults hold the power to help lessen its effects. Several factors can change the course of kids' lives: feeling seen and heard by a caring adult, being patiently taught coping strategies and resilience-building techniques, and being with adults who know about the effects of such experiences. Here are ways to bring these factors to life.

Learning Disabilities

NICHCY (http://nichcy.org/families-community)

NICHCY serves the nation as a central source of information on disabilities in infants, toddlers, children and youth. You'll find easy-to-read articles on IDEA, the law authorizing early intervention services and special education, as well as researched-based information on effective practices, programs and services.

Easterseals (http://www.easterseals.com/)

For nearly 100 years, Easterseals has been the indispensable resource for people and families challenged by disability. Now, as America faces a broad range of new issues, we make a major, positive, life—changing difference in the lives of people and families challenged by today's disabilities. The work we do every day is redefining disability for the 21st century.

Child Development Institute (http://childdevelopmentinfo.com/)

Our website is designed to provide the information and tools parents need to understand their unique child/children and to enable them to help each child develop into the successful human being they were meant to be.

Through the Looking Glass (http://www.lookingglass.org/)

Through the Looking Glass (TLG) is a nationally-recognized center that has pioneered research, training and services for families in which a child, parent or grandparent has a disability or medical issue. Our mission is "To create, demonstrate and encourage non-pathological and empowering resources and model early intervention services for families with disability issues in parent or child which integrate expertise derived from personal disability experience and disability culture."

PACER (http://www.pacer.org/)

The mission of PACER Center (Parent Advocacy Coalition for Educational Rights) is to expand opportunities and enhance the quality of life of children and young adults with disabilities and their families, based on the concept of parents helping parents. With assistance to individual families, workshops, materials for parents and professionals and leadership in securing a free and appropriate public education for all children, PACER's work affects and encourages families in Minnesota and across the nation.

Parents Helping Parents (http://www.php.com/)

Parents Helping Parents (PHP) strives to improve the quality of life for any child with any special need of any age, through educating, supporting and training their primary caregivers.

E-Ready Special Education Information for Parents (http://www.pta.org/advocacy/content.cfm?ItemNumber=3713)

This page provides parents, as well as teachers, of children with disabilities with information on specific disabilities, a glossary of special education terms, and links to helpful resources.

AllExperts – Special Education (http://www.allexperts.com/cl2/636/education/Special-Education/)

This website allows parents to ask questions of AllExpert's volunteer experts regarding all aspects of special education; questions and answers are available for search as well.

U.S. Department of Education (http://www2.ed.gov/parents/needs/speced/edpicks.jhtml)

The Department of Education provides a list of resources pertaining to the needs of children with disabilities.

Understood (www.understood.org)

Their goal is to help the millions of parents whose children, ages 3–20, are struggling with learning and attention issues. They provide a wealth of information to help educators and parents understand their children's issues and relate to their experiences.

Teacher Resources

National Association of Special Education Teachers (http://www.naset.org/)

NASET is the premier membership organization for special education teachers and offers a wealth of resources, including professional development courses, job postings, and more.

U.S. Department of Education Strengthening Teaching (http://www.ed.gov/teaching)

Articles and resources for educators.

Stop Bullying Teacher Guide (http://www.stopbullying.gov/what-you-can-do/educators/index.html)

Helping to establish a supportive and safe school climate where all students are accepted and knowing how to respond when bullying happens are key to making sure all students are able to learn and grow. There are many tools on StopBullying.gov specific for teachers, administrators and other school staff.

The Council for Learning Disabilities (CLD) (http://www.cldinternational.org)

The Council for Learning Disabilities is an international organization that promotes evidence-based teaching, collaboration, research, leadership and advocacy. CLD is comprised of professionals who represent diverse disciplines and are committed to enhancing the education and quality of life for individuals with learning disabilities and others who experience challenges in learning.

Teaching LD (http://teachingld.org/)

Information and resources for teaching students with learning disabilities. The Division for Learning Disabilities (DLD) is one of 17 special interest groups of the Council for Exceptional Children (CEC), the largest international professional organization dedicated to improving educational outcomes for individuals with exceptionalities, including both students with disabilities and the gifted.

I'm Determined (https://www.imdetermined.org)

The I'm Determined project, a state-directed project funded by the Virginia Department of Education, focuses on providing direct instruction, models, and opportunities to practice skills associated with self-determined behavior. This project facilitates youth, especially those with disabilities to undertake a measure of control in their lives, helping to set and steer the course rather than remaining the silent passenger.

Emotional and behavioral disorders

National Federation of Families for Children's Mental Health (FFCMH) (http://www.ffcmh.org)

The National Federation of Families for Children's Mental Health is a national family-run organization linking more than 120 chapters and state organizations focused on the issues of children and youth with emotional, behavioral or mental health needs and their families.

American Academy of Child and Adolescent Psychiatry (AACAP) (http://www.aacap.org/aacap/Families_and_Youth/Facts_for_Families/Home.aspx)

The AACAP developed Facts for Families to provide concise and up-to-date information on psychiatric issues that affect children, teenagers and their families. The AACAP provides this important information as a public service.

National Alliance on Mental Illness (NAMI) (http://www.nami.org)

NAMI is the National Alliance on Mental Illness, the nation's largest grassroots mental health organization dedicated to building better lives for the millions of Americans affected by mental illness. NAMI advocates for access to services, treatment, supports and research and is steadfast in its commitment to raise awareness and build a community for hope for all of those in need.

Attention Deficit Disorder/Attention-Deficit/Hyperactivity Disorder

CHADD (http://www.chadd.org/)

Children and Adults with Attention-Deficit/Hyperactivity Disorder (CHADD), is a national non-profit, tax-exempt organization providing education, advocacy and support for individuals with ADHD. In addition to our informative website, CHADD also publishes a variety of printed materials to keep members and professionals current on research advances, medications and treatments affecting individuals with ADHD.

KidSource Online (http://www.kidsource.com/kidsource/pages/dis.add.html)

KidSource Online is a group of parents who want to make a positive and lasting difference in the lives of parents and children. We've brought together our best articles in the Disabilities: Attention Deficit Disorder section of our website. Information on learning disabilities and physical disabilities can be found in other sections.

The Attention Deficit Disorder Association (http://www.add.org/)

The Attention Deficit Disorder Association provides information, resources and networking opportunities to help adults with Attention Deficit Hyperactivity Disorder lead better lives.

One Add Place (http://www.oneaddplace.com/)

At the ADD and ADHD resource place you will find information on both child and adult attention deficit disorder and attention deficit hyperactivity disorder. Learn the symptoms of ADD and ADHD and how to test for them, and discover the latest natural treatments, pharmaceutical medications and brain science.

Legal/advocacy information and resources

National Disability Rights Network (http://www.ndrn.org/index.php)

Every single day, our Network protects and advocates for the rights of people with disabilities across the United States and the territories. We fight to end abuse and neglect where we find it. We assist people in finding and keeping their jobs and work with kids, parents and schools to combat bullying and ensure educational opportunities for students with disabilities.

Education Law Resource Center (http://www.edlawrc.com/)

The Education Law Resource Center provides information to help parents, educators and other professionals understand legal requirements and meet student needs. This site contains information and resources about a variety of education law topics including physical restraints in schools, special education and No Child Left Behind.

The Individuals with Disabilities Education Act (http://idea.ed.gov/)

The official website of the Individuals with Disabilities Education Act (IDEA), Part B (ages 3 to 21) and Part C (birth to 2 years).

Visual Impairment

FamilyConnect (http://www.familyconnect.org/parentsitehome.asp)

FamilyConnect is designed for parents of children with visual impairments, and brought to you by American Foundation for the Blind and National Association for Parents of Children with Visual Impairments. On FamilyConnect you'll find videos, personal stories, events, news and an online community that can offer tips and support from other parents of children who are blind or visually impaired.

The National Association for Parents of Children with Visual Impairments (NAPVI) (http://www.napvi.org/)

NAPVI is a non-profit organization of, by and for parents committed to providing support to the parents of children who have visual impairments. NAPVI is a national organization that enables parents to find information and resources for their children who are blind or visually impaired, including those with additional disabilities.

Gangs

Help Starts Here (www.helpstartshere.org)

It is a website where social workers offer tips for parents, teachers and children regarding issues relating to adolescent development, mental health issues, etc.

National Gang Crime Research Center (www.ngcrc.com)

It is a non-profit independent agency that promotes research, disseminates information, and provides training and consultation services regarding gangs, gang members and gang problems.

National Crime Intelligence Resource Center (www.ncirc.gov)

It is a program of the Bureau of Justice Assistance/U.S. Department of Justice that aims at reducing and preventing crime, violence, and drug abuse and improving the criminal justice system.

Books

Books (http://www.tfcbooks.org/)

Teaching for Change (TFC) carefully selects booklists that highlight titles by and about people of color as well as social justice themes.

We Need Diverse Books (WNDB) (http://weneeddiversebooks.org/)

WNDB is dedicated to highlighting the best of diverse literature for children and teens and to heightening awareness through continued education.

www.ingramcontent.com/pod-product-compliance
Lightning Source LLC
Chambersburg PA
CBHW042002150426
43194CB00002B/96